Things Live After

poems by

Carol Nolde

Finishing Line Press
Georgetown, Kentucky

Things Live After

Copyright © 2018 by Carol Nolde
ISBN 978-1-63534-438-7 First Edition
All rights reserved under International and Pan-American Copyright Conventions.
No part of this book may be reproduced in any manner whatsoever without written permission from the publisher, except in the case of brief quotations embodied in critical articles and reviews.

ACKNOWLEDGMENTS

Grateful acknowledgment is made to the following journals in which these poems have appeared:

Adirondac : "On His Own"
Architrave : "A Lost Duchess"
Array : "Not Like Dick and Jane"
Blueline : "Going Home," "Connected"
Broadkill Review: "The Saved"
Child of My Child: "Now a Mother"
Cyclamensandswords.com "Land of the Heart," "Then and Now"
Earth's Daughters: "Things Live After Us"
Ekphrasis: "Fox Hunt," "Bright Light at Russell's Corners"
Exit 13: "Sahara Dark," "Varanasi, Night Ride," "Obsolescence"
Knowing Stones: Poems of Exotic Places: "Horus' Eye"
Miramar: "Five Women" in press
Newark Review: "Civility"
Off Line, An Anthology of New Jersey Poets: "Mysteries"
Salonika: "Dream of Spain"
The MacGuffin : "Mother and Child"
U.S.1 Worksheets: "Storm," "Tiger Hour," "Identity" in press
Voices of Israel 2015: "At Auschwitz, In a Display Case," "Unclaimed"
Whetstone: "In the Artist's Hand"

Publisher: Leah Maines
Editor: Christen Kincaid
Cover Art: Photograph of the family homestead built by the author's great grandfather in 1902.
Author Photo: Frank Nolde
Cover Design: Elizabeth Maines McCleavy

Printed in the USA on acid-free paper.
Order online: www.finishinglinepress.com
        also available on amazon.com

Author inquiries and mail orders:
Finishing Line Press
P. O. Box 1626
Georgetown, Kentucky 40324
U. S. A.

Table of Contents

Things Live After Us 1
Five Women 2
The Saved 3
Going Home 5
Obsolescence 6
Storm 7
Fox Hunt 8
Not Like Dick and Jane 9
Connected 10
"Bright Light at Russell's Corners, 1946" 11
Land of the Heart 12
In the Artist's Hand 13
A Lost Duchess 14
Mother and Child 115
On His Own 16
Dream of Spain 18
Unclaimed 19
Now a Mother 20
At Auschwitz, in a Display Case 21
Mysteries 22
Tiger Hour 23
Varanasi, Night Ride 24
Identity 25
Finisterra 26
Horus' Eye 27
Sahara Dark 29
Civility 30
Then and Now 31

For Frank

Things Live after Us
For my friend R.V.

Things live after us:
the wheel rutted streets of Pompeii,
the fetal curve in hardened lava of child and dog,
the photograph of you posed at the ancient grindstone
to show your students how it once turned.
History teacher, you dealt in artifacts
your classroom walls papered with the past
the framed Acropolis and Forum, reminders that
the White House and Pentagon unpeopled
will not tell our story.

The house is emptied.
Men worked in the dark.
The kitchen table, heavy with dishes, stands on the lawn.
The blue teapot saved on the back shelf,
its gold banding bright as your wedding day,
joins the cracked cups and chipped saucers white in the morning sun.
In the grass the cord of the kitchen clock dangles.
At the auctioneer's block,
books from the shelves next to your bed, boxed.
Soon strange eyes will scan the titles,
note your name printed on bookplates or scrawled inside covers,
and when the gavel pounds,
all the words you couldn't live without will scatter
like dandelion parachutes in the wind.

Five Women
        at the town book sale

From a folding table marked "fiction,"
I picked up *Middlemarch*, not to buy,
but simply to run my hand over, open
as if greeting an old friend. The genie

that rose was a name I knew, inked
in perfect Palmer on a card once marking
her place: to Laura from Kate, Florida,
Christmas, three decades ago.

Then both were my age, Laura, not dead,
her books still on her library shelves,
and Kate, years away from the nursing home
where she lives cocooned in a muffled world.

Growing up, I felt these women held the secret
to all that is printed in books. I loved the way
they talked grammatically, used words I'd never heard.
Kate was the mother of my best friend,

who made me promise not to tell
the times her mother was sent away.
When Kate came back, she sold dresses,
and chatted with customers in the family store.

Laura taught third grade and when she retired,
separated from her lumberjack husband,
then took trips to England and the continent.
On the December day the card arrived from Florida,

I picture Laura, wrapped in a wool afghan,
lost in Dorothea's world, but aware
that snow drifts just beyond the pane.
Kate's words, slipped between the pages, press into Eliot's.
Silent as remembered voices—the women.

The Saved
Anglo-Saxon lines—after Richard Wilbur

Attic trunks talked
    whispered, "Touch me.
Spring the latch,
    and lift the dome. Look."
Like Alice I listened,
    lifted weighty lids.
Once there lay lace,
    fragrance of lavender
Faint in the folds
    that unfanned between my fingers.
Beneath, bolts
    of cambric, banded by
Borders embroidered
    with a bride's bold initial
Pure white
    waiting, still.

    *

Cast-off clothes
    cluttered the closet
Bent the boxes
    they balanced above
Pressed postcards
    preserved between pages
Their scrawled messages
    strangely short.
Snapshots never sorted
    by subject or date
Black and white, some bent
    others blurry.
Though none were labeled,
    I knew some and named them
Noted the number
    now anonymous.

*

A letter had lain long
                in a leather
Folder frayed
                and flattened.
Caught in its crease
                a curl of hair
Brown as the braid
                I held it beside.
"Dear daughter," it began,
                "Diana drifted off
as we stood by
                singing her favorite psalm.
We buried her
                beside brother.
Keep faith.
                Your loving father, Philip."

*

Such scattered segments
                salvaged scraps
Like archaeological
                artifacts
Defy death
                dare us
To find in fragments
                the full figure of a life
Press us for proof
                of pattern and purpose.

Going Home

Nearing the road that once led home
an impulse urged the wheel to turn in the old
direction, follow the rain between folds
of fields once farmed, now woods. Only the stones
stacked to mark boundaries spoke like tombs
of the work of those who tried to hold
the power of nature back, knowing control
was never theirs. The homestead loomed
as it always had, a ship in the sea of dark.
So I could almost believe if my tires crackled
over cinders from winters of ice, a barking
dog would rouse the dead who lived in the ramshackle
house, and someone, a coat draping his head,
would step from the porch, offer warmth and a bed.

Obsolescence
> "Old barns are as obsolete as the manual typewriter in the computer age."
> John Berdo, a seventh generation farmer, The New York Times

The land seems barren when a barn disappears.
On the hill opposite ours where Kimball's fell,
my eye fills the blank that for a hundred years
or more was a family farm. There I knelt
in a field to pick wild strawberries, so ruby
ripe my fingers stained with their essence. When trees
had taken back those fields, the barn stayed
though it seemed to grow smaller and darker as it decayed
on the hill opposite ours before it fell.

Half the country's wooden barns are lost
whose hand-pegged beams once held
cattle and horses and hay forked into lofts.
Livestock and machines too large for a barn
are housed today in metal sheds. No fear
once real that fire will devastate a farm.
The land seems barren when a barn disappears.

Storm

Snow clung to your denim jacket like the smell
of cattle as I kissed your cold, unshaven cheek.
Across the red linoleum, your boots leaked
rivers. I laughed as you began to tell
of tunneling to the stable. The stove had cast its spell
as you rubbed chapped hands. Though wind shrieked
in the chimney, wood shifted and the house creaked,
it seemed there was nothing that warmth could not repel.

Snow outlines the field's stubbled rows
and frozen tracks, plasters the trunks of trees,
edges the barn's weathered red to enclose
all in white. The sky does not relieve
the threat of night that's setting out to reclaim
the earth, of drifts against granite obliterating your name.

Fox Hunt
      on a painting by Winslow Homer (1836-1910)

Half-buried in snow, Homer's name rises
black on white in the painting's left corner.
At the center a red fox sinks, belly deep
in the drift, one paw upraised in labored flight
from black beaks hovering so close
the snow silent air beats with their cries.
Hunger has driven him to the edge of the dark
sea that foams against gray rocks.
Everything is buried but a wild rose bush
one bough above the drift, bent
with ruby hips the wind will whip until they drop.

Not Like Dick and Jane

The odor of our wool mittens drying by the stove
rose with the dough spilling over the bowl's rim,
mingled with scent of cinnamon and clove from spice cake.
My mother's yoked print apron white with flour
stretched across her belly rounding below her breasts.
Her stubby fingers shaped even rounds of dough,
pressed them in threes like clover leaves in greased tins--
such precision present nowhere in her life,
the product of her hands, not her mind, which beat against
the panes of light, shrieked like crows over torn flesh.
But Saturdays the cookie jars, bread box, and cake
tins swelled with bounty she'd stirred and shaped and baked.
If only we could have pressed our heads against her aproned
belly, brushed the flour from her cheek to plant a kiss.
Instead when our toes warmed, we shoved our feet into boots
still damp, pulled on steaming mittens,
and raced into the cold.

Connected

"Farmhouse for sale" the billboard blares
then lists the towns where anyone with money
can find a perfect place for country living.
So Uncle Len's and Matt's, then Willie's sold
to people who had no way of knowing the life
and death that happened there in space they now
began to rearrange to make their own.

Antique shops, boutiques, and galleries line
the street where once a week farm wives
shopped for groceries at Cousin Jenny's store.
The farmers went to Beck's for whatever they couldn't
find at home: bins of nails, nuts,
and bolts, boots, hats, overalls, linaments.
If it wasn't out, John found it in the back.

Men have scraped and painted Jenny's and Beck's,
hung signs: "Tanning Salon," "Mountain Antiques."
The windows are clean again, the walks swept,
and pots of flowers bloom beside the doors.
Shoppers can find quilts to hang on walls,
egg pails painted white for magazines,
and milk cans with decals to decorate a doorway.

Uncle Willie's porch no longer sags,
his rocker replaced by white wicker. Here
warm evenings, he and Aunt Rose had sat
to watch fireflies signal above the fields.
The house is air conditioned now and the owners,
their faces lit blue by the t.v.'s beamed messages,
no longer are isolated between the earth and sky.

"Bright Light at Russell's Corners, 1946"
"To Make a World: George Ault and 1940's America"
Smithsonian American Art Museum, May, 2011

Ault knew the dark of country roads
how suddenly a road can bend, send a car floating
free out over a lake like Icarus
before his descent, swallowed without a trace.
So the artist was drawn to the bright light at Russell's Corners,
the way it illumined the side of a red barn in need of paint,
signaled the need to slow down on the right-angled macadam.

Ault's widow told of the way he ordered his studio
put everything in place before he could begin to work,
perfect as the white building in this painting that hugs
the road's edge, its clapboards narrow and straight.
Opposite, in silhouette a derelict split-rail fence
surrounds a dark field that needs mowing.

Power lines, lit gold, score the sky, emphasize
the dark of a country night without moon or stars.
Only the light at Russell's Corners keeps
the stranger's car around the hairpin turn
known to locals, but the light beckons to all who travel
an otherwise dark road, reminds them that maybe
cattle are bedded in the barn and inside the house someone sleeps.

Land of the Heart

> *Paintings of Adriaen Coorte (active 1683-1707)   ~National Gallery of Art*
> *"The poem...can be a message inside a bottle, sent out in the not always secure belief that it could be washed ashore somewhere, sometime, perhaps on a land of the heart..." ~Paul Celan*

The texture is so exact that we can see
the cut ends of the asparagus starting to dry
and the individual xylem appear.
Fibers of the frayed cord around
them are visible against their white flesh.
Light from an unseen window illumines
wet red currants that hang from the table's edge,
silvers the tips of their dark velvet leaves.
Wild strawberries heaped in a Chinese bowl,
chestnuts strewn on a cracked stone ledge,
seashells, peaches, gooseberries.

Nothing is known of the artist who signed and dated
these small still lifes except
he sold them in Zeeland for a meager sum.
Today in the gallery, crowds press to study
the simple objects caught in the light of a dark world.
No words tell the painter's thoughts.
But in the translucent beauty of gooseberries,
the perfection of the strawberry blossom that will not last,
we can only guess what drives an artist
back and back again is desire
somehow to get the vision right.

In the Artist's Hand
Mary Cassatt exhibit, the Museum of Fine Arts, Boston

Cassatt's pastels, chalks of no particular
brilliance, broken, not what one would expect
in a master's hand, encased and labeled, a curiosity
below the portraits.
                    Such a meagre store
to capture the sheen of leg-of-mutton sleeves
so that we feel the yellow silk beneath
the child's hand, the peach roundness of the cheek
the mother's face is buried in. Which sticks
of color could have blent to fix the shimmer
of red-gold hair and hint of brows
above the eyes so blue the whites appear
blue too, the gaze assured safe
from the noise and notice of the world? The moment's private
when the mother's lips have met her child's cheek,
the child pressed against familiar warmth
that glows pink to red along the lobe,
exposed by the sweep of hair into a bun,
a roundness complete as the sleeve encircling the child.

As a writer's words lying flat and black
sometimes will rise above their ordered lines,
her chalks illumine a world that defies a frame.

A Lost Duchess

"If you could choose a painter for your portrait,
who would it be?" he questioned over lunch.
They'd seen so many women caught by men
on canvas, she paused, her fork mid-air and looked
into his laughing eyes and wondered how
he'd like to see her done.
                        Perhaps as pink
cheeked Artemis in bosom baring gown
of rustling silk, one ribbon tied about
the whiteness of her throat. Her bow, the only
sign that she is goddess of the hunt.
"With the children?" she asked.
                              "It's up to you," he smiled.
She saw herself a Sargent duchess--languid,
the arms of her diaphanous gown like wings
along the damasked sofa back encircling
her children, dressed in white, her ringed fingers
caressing golden curls against her breast.

"I think I'll have the portrait just of me."
She knew the way she wished to be remembered
and who could capture truth about her best.
She saw the background dark, its details spare,
the light oblique upon her figure, plainly dressed,
her hands at rest upon her lap, blue ridged,
red knuckled, unadorned. Her eyes, like opals,
catch the light. In them, the painter reads
her life and leaves it for the world to see.

Her husband leaned across the table, "Well?"
Although she feared her choice would disappoint
because he loved the grandeur of the past,
she softly said, "It must be Thomas Eakins."

Mother and Child
    on a painting by Cecilia Beaux (1863-1942)

Gowned in black, she sits in profile, her head
bent over her child, who rests against
her breast. He's tired from play or maybe half
asleep just risen from a nap. Perhaps
she's been away. Are those her gloves on the table
near them? He's missed her comfort all day.
Her eyes seem closed, the way a purring cat's
see all through slits. Her arms encircling him,
cannot contain the sturdy legs that dangle
from his dress of ruffled white and might
without a moment's notice send him sliding
from her silken lap. For now, he feels
the steady rhythm of her breath, her fragrant
warmth beneath his body pressed to hers.
There with her, he dares to stare at us,
who stand outside the private space they share,
and at the world that he will leave her for.

On His Own

At dusk we waited---almost able to measure
the passing season by the sun's earlier setting
further west. Light was his clock
and as it left, his head appeared above
the window frame, a black lump that hunched
over the edge (I swore that once I saw
his toes curl around the frame) poised
as if to survey the scene before he dropped,
but as in dreams of falling, propelled his way
up and out long before he hit
the porch floor and floated over the rail.

We called him "he" because he was alone---
he suckled none. Droppings from only one
fell below the window or streaked the stucco.
Despite the mess, I felt somehow privileged
he'd chosen shelter within our walls. Some
people put up boxes to lure bats,
but ours just found us. I remember
when I was a child, a bat, blinded by light,
battered against our kitchen ceiling until
my father, swinging wildly, hit him,
then carried away the tiny body, lifeless
on the back of a broom. Only recently I read
mysterious deaths by rabies are caused by bats.
A girl camping with her family died untreated
because no one knew she'd been bitten.

I think of our bat clinging to the wall of a cave
probably somewhere in Virginia where so many winter
and wonder where he'll live when he returns
to find his home filled in. We'll probably
see him in the orchard along with all the others
who skim above the trees, silhouettes against
a darkening sky, but we won't know which
one he is, and like a child once
they no longer live under the family roof,
he won't be ours.

Dream of Spain

If I were a wave lapping Coruña's rocky harbor,
maybe I'd catch a glimpse of you hurrying to work
down the pink, palm-lined sidewalk,
but it wouldn't satisfy me any more
than the vibrations over air that register
your voice in my ear. No,   I'll be a cat,
one of dozens among the stones that feed
on water rats and fish scraps tossed from boats.

In my disguise, I'll be   Marmalade,
the tabby you mothered when you were ten,
who taught you the pain of separation.
Reincarnated, I'll crawl from between the stones,
startle your memory in my orange and white coat.
You will bend, croon to win my confidence.
I will sniff your open palm, press my warmth
against your legs, weave a circle around you.

Surprised, you'll pick me up, call me "Kitty,"
and I will nuzzle your ear and neck knowing
the scent beyond soap, sure that it is you.

Unclaimed
At the Florence Foundling Hospital

We swaddled our first born child
in soft, sweet smelling flannel.
Waving her arms and legs, she would look up
from the center of the cloth diamond
as her father folded her into its warmth,
placing one point over her legs and stomach
drawing the other two over the first
tucking them firmly under her body.

I see her in the Della Robbia reliefs
above the hospital's colonnaded porch,
terra cotta cherubs, porcelain-white
looking down from sky-blue roundels.
Most have lower bodies swaddled, though some
have wiggled free, the blanket dropped back
to reveal the sex. Arms opened wide,
they accept all who ascend the steps.

I wonder if a mother who entered here raised her eyes
and saw their smiling beauty or was she blinded by grief,
by fear that this would be the last she would see
trust in her baby's eyes, feel his breath
against her neck. Soon she must leave,
place him within the horizontal wheel
that would rotate him away into the building.
Then she could leave unseen.

But first she must record his identity.
How carefully she must have tied the ribbon around his ankle,
so returning, she could say, "The child with a green ribbon,
'Eduardo' embroidered in white."

Here in a case, mothers' last gifts,
identity affixed to the child they hoped to reclaim:
a silver bell, a glass scent bottle,
a strand of beads, a cross with red stones.

Now a Mother

It's the way my daughter's arm encircles
her baby, whose bare back bends
toward the sand and waves that lap
at her mother's feet, her tiny
buttocks resting on the arm beneath her.

It's the way my daughter's body leans
toward the water, wanting the child to feel
the pull of sand and sea,
but only so much,
as someday she'll urge her
to greet an admiring stranger,
but hold her hand.

It's the way
their flesh meets
arm, buttocks, hand
the way I still long to touch the back
bent above the child,
want to hold them both,
knowing the bond that joins, separates.

At Auschwitz, in a Display Case

Pale blue, handknit in the finest wool,
the kind of baby sweater seen only in exclusive
shops, but here among these artifacts,
I picture the young woman who sat by a window to knit.
The light touches her hair, the rows of stitches
that grow above her rounded belly, or maybe
it's her mother, longing to hold a child after many years.
The sweater, she feels, makes the future real.
She can almost see the blue eyes like her daughter's,
imagine the sweet scent of the body against her shoulder,
the neck she will nuzzle.   When word comes
that they must leave, she helps her daughter pack
and in bold letters labels the suitcase KIND.
Is the sweater folded inside or did they struggle
to put the tiny arms in sleeves, a layer
he will need against the coming cold?
And when the guard commands, "Form two lines,"
does she offer to hold the child because she knows
the old and very young are sure to die?

Kind, the German word for child

Mysteries

Her baby in one arm, the other she extends, hand cupped,
then raised to press her fingertips against her lips.
On the temple road, clad in white tunic and white turban,
a supplicant casts himself full length on the pavement.
At each step he drops and rises, drops and rises.
Workmen on scaffolds wash the Empress' marble tomb.
A pool doubles the glistening dome, white against blue
as ox-drawn mowers perfume the air.

Only men accompany the dead, descend the river ghat
to carry the litter into the purifying water of the Ganges.
In the light of pyres, the golden shroud glitters.
Each day the mother and baby stand in diesel exhaust.
She raises her cupped hand toward a bus window,
then presses her fingertips against her lips.
The man in white labors toward Rathambore.
He believes he must reach the steep on his knees by holy day.

Thousands of men worked over twenty years at the Emperor's
        command,
raised a monument of perfect symmetry, fashioned with inlays
of marble, yellow and black, red stone from Fatehpur Sikri.
The air in Varanasi hangs heavy with smoke.
The sick and the dying have come here to bathe in the holy river,
send flower-laden candles adrift on the current.
The mother extends her cupped hand, then presses her lips with her
        fingertips.
Even protected in white gloves the penitent's hands bleed, raw.

Tiger Hour
Rathambore, India

No fear in the inexperienced, the young deer
grazed their way across the plain in morning peace.
But when a few antlered heads suddenly rose
even the peacocks stood at attention,
followed their gaze beyond the watering hole
into the tall grass. High-powered binoculars
could not perceive the presence that for a moment held
all. Then drawn back to the familiar, they fed.

For over an hour we watched, spoke in hushed
voices, if at all, waited with them
for what seemed the inevitable. Would the morning end
in flight or would one young or old and frail,
who cropped sweet grass in early light, fight
to live? Like a gun sounding the start of a race,
a samba deer snorted an alarm that scattered life
away from the parting grass where Death emerged.
One swipe of its terrible paw could have felled
any but the strongest. But speed or luck saved all
and Death lay down, for the moment thwarted.

Varanasi, Night Ride

The boatman rowed us over the river
famous for the dead burning on its banks
the corpses that sink into its dark
then rise to lift an arm or hand
curled toward the boats and votives
floating on the sacred road.

He kept us a "respectful distance," he said,
from the relatives carrying litters draped in gold
down the steep ghat toward the water.
Logs rolled from piles that line the bank
become a pyre for the body's ascension
through gray air and the odor of burning flesh.

Over the black water we sent votives.
No one spoke as we neared the shore.
Past the hungry eyes of a legless beggar,
children's open palms, we climbed stairs
toward rickshaws and the men who would carry us
weighted by all we had seen.

Identity
> *Rijks Museum, Amsterdam*
> *17th century Dutch whalers' caps from graves near Spitsbergen,*
> *Norway, opened in 1980*

When their bodies were exhumed, the Dutchmen
still wore their knitted woolen caps.
Three hundred years undisturbed
in private dark. If they now could rise,
they'd be hailed by fellow whalers, recognized
by stripes and colors that individualized
the caps that clung to skulls that neither wife
nor mother could rightly claim for certain as her own.

Bundled against fierce cold, only their eyes
visible, they knew each other by green stripe,
or orange band knit by women whose hands
were powerless against the storms they knew would come.
Aware each voyage could be their last,
the men packed wood to build their coffins,
perhaps some moss on which to rest their feet.
And when a body was prepared for burial in foreign soil,
a cap was drawn over the round of the nameless head,
the cap that set each man apart,
the cap that said, this is he.

Finisterra
> *Spain*

Where the sea hurls itself against land's end
a church rises from rock, a beacon,
not to sailors, but to those they left.

Through its thick closed door, the roar
of sea and wind drowns the human voice,
rocks the rafters where votive ships sway.

Knees turn cold on stones that line the aisle;
above bent heads, the tiny vessels
voyage, heavy with hope or grief.

Horus' Eye

So many forties' films begin on trains--
The camera focuses on a woman's white legs
crossed beneath a smart suit, maybe
a veil falling from a hat set at an angle
to cover thick lashed eyes above
a full, dark mouth we know must be red.
Opposite, a man barks words and smoke
between a narrow line of lips--his eyes
slits from smoke or stealth take her in.
In truth, I'm hatless in a flowered skirt beside
my husband, who also doesn't look the part,
but here we are skimming across the desert.

The tick of the rails, steady as an old projector
on rewind, takes us past the black and white reel
to ancient times that flicker in the frame of our window,
but the women who kneel on the banks are real.
Not posed in prayer, they bend to the Nile
to dip the clothes they rub against rocks
while a *shadoof* lifts a bucket for white robed
men who feed the green they've planted in rows
along the banks. Sometimes a donkey
driven circle after circle turns
a wheel that raises river to field,
Archimedes' modern way to water.

Horus' Eye, 2

We are headed south against the current
to the Aswan Dam that does not allow
the north flowing Nile to flood its banks,
instead transforms its force to light.
As the train moves forward taking us back
toward the river's source, I stare
at people bent over work
that has not changed though centuries have passed.
They only glance at the silver snake that slides
along the rail and at our faces framed in glass.
They do not know that film winds behind
my eyes, records the silent mystery of their lives

so when our plane rises above the desert
brown, I will look down into the muddy river
racing between strips of green and unreel
a past that lies beyond all living memory.

Sahara Dark

The tent zipper's squawk and my circle of light
intrude on the black silence. I hold my breath.
Listen. No sound. I move in stealth
toward a tent I know is there though my sight
cannot confirm it. In such a night
I can believe the universe would weather
the loss of human life, even the death
of our galaxy and the billions beyond. Our matter is slight,
four percent, I've read; the rest is dark,
unknown for now and possibly forever.
Disoriented and lost in the cold and dark, I shiver
but stop to marvel at the shower of stars that arc
above my head. The rest is mystery mass
I will never know beyond this bliss.

Civility

Today thousands of people converged on the lawn
for Mozart. After the last gong
of the summoning bell, an expectant silence fell,
so ears could accept the first note.
Under puffs of cloud adrift in blue
the heart opens as it cannot
under crystal chandeliers gone dim
above dark rows where pages rustle
and coughs strain behind cupped hands.
Here, two ten year old boys weave among blankets.
One with finger to lips checks the other, already silent,
before they settle under a yellow umbrella.
Even the two year old in pink-checked pinafore,
playing with her mother's sandals, is part of the silent story
each blanket or cluster of webbed chairs could tell,
but differences here are subsumed. We attend the piano
that sings to winds and strings, gives voice
to questions no words can still.
The music tries and in the space it fills,
we listen.

Then and Now

With My Grandmother

June found them on their knees. They had to creep
across the field careful not to crush
the berry carpet, ripe, red, lush.
The child soon learned the pressure to keep

between thumb and forefinger to free
the tiny berry, not lose its essence in a gush.
She matched her grandmother's rhythm, no rush.
Patience, she saw, is the way to reap

and slowly the empty pail will fill.
Even time seemed to creep in the hush of heat,
a canopy that hung over the flat, still
field. A bell might sound from a cow nearly asleep
in shade of fencerow trees. In sun
held by their work, woman and child were one.

With My Granddaughter

She looks at me in question, presses a blueberry
against her lips. I smile and nod my head.
We work our way around the bush: the very
bottom hers, the top mine. A thread

unravels. I am led into a labyrinth
where a child and her grandmother still live.
Once the empty pail had daunted me, no hint
that it would overflow. The day outlives

the hours spent in the sunfilled field,
stored like a jar of garnet in secret dark,
the scent of strawberries in sun, sealed.
On a morning when frost rimes tree bark,
we will tap our rich store,
savor a sweetness we had not known before.

Additional Acknowledgments

Special thanks to Deena Linett, Charlotte Mandel, Emily Fragos, Molly Peacock, and Marie Ponsot for their friendship, support, and sharing a life in poetry.

Carol Nolde and her husband live in Westfield, New Jersey, where she taught English and creative writing and for many years was an associate editor for Merlyn's Pen, a national magazine of teenage writers.

She and her family spend part of each year in Sullivan County, New York, in the foothills of the Catskills, where her ancestors settled in the early 19th century. She grew up in the house her great-grandparents built on the land cleared for farming by her great-great grandparents, immigrants from Ireland. The photograph on the cover of *Things Live After* shows the family celebrating the home's completion in 1902. Nolde's poetry reflects a life steeped in family history and the history of the region.

She is the author of the chapbook *Comfort in Stone* (Finishing Line Press, 2014). Her poems have appeared in many publications including the anthologies *Knowing Stones: Poems of Exotic Places*, the second edition of *Love Is Ageless-Stories About Alzheimer's Disease, Child of My Child, Joys of the Table,* and *Forgotten Women.*

www.ingramcontent.com/pod-product-compliance
Lightning Source LLC
LaVergne TN
LVHW041558070426
835507LV00011B/1166